Explore History

ANCIENT EGYPT

JANE SHUTER

Heinemann

H www.heinemann.co.uk
Visit our website to find out more information about Heinemann books.

To order:
☎ Phone 44 (0) 1865 888020
📄 Send a fax to 44 (0) 1865 314091
💻 Visit the Heinemann Bookshop at www.heinemann.co.uk to browse our catalogue and order online.

First published in Great Britain by Heinemann Library, Halley Court, Jordan Hill, Oxford OX2 8EJ, a division of Reed Educational and Professional Publishing Ltd. Heinemann is a registered trademark of Reed Educational & Professional Publishing Ltd.

OXFORD MELBOURNE AUCKLAND JOHANNESBURG BLANTYRE
GABORONE IBADAN PORTSMOUTH (NH) USA CHICAGO

© Reed Educational and Professional Publishing Ltd 2001
The moral right of the proprietor has been asserted.

Designed by Celia Floyd
Illustrations by Jeff Edwards
Originated by Dot Gradations
Printed in Hong Kong

05 04 03 02 01   05 04 03 02
10 9 8 7 6 5 4 3 2 1   10 9 8 7 6 5 4 3
ISBN 0 431 10206 6 (hardback)   ISBN 0 431 10215 5 (paperback)

British Library Cataloguing in Publication Data

Shuter, Jane
  Ancient Egypt. – (Explore History)
  1.Egypt – History – To 332 B.C. 2.Egypt – Civilization – To 332 B.C.
  3.Egypt – Social life and customs – To 332 B.C.
  I. Title
  932'.01

Acknowledgements

The Publishers would like to thank the following for permission to reproduce photographs:

Ashmolean Museum: pg.12, pg.17; British Museum; pg.16, pg.20, pg.29; Christine Osborne: pg.21; Corbis: pg.11; Hilary Fletcher: pg.10, pg.19, pg.28; Phil Cooke & Magnet Harlequin: pg.5, pg.15, pg.18, pg.20, pg.22, pg.25, pg.26, pg.27; Photo Archive: pg.14; Trip: pg.9; Werner Forman Archive: pg.7, pg.13, pg.23, pg.24.

Cover photograph reproduced with permission of Michael Holford.

Every effort has been made to contact copyright holders of any material reproduced in this book. Any omissions will be rectified in subsequent printings if notice is given to the Publisher.

Any words appearing in the text in bold, **like this**, are explained in the glossary.

Contents

What do we already know about ancient Egypt?

The ancient Egyptian civilization lasted from about 3100 BC to the Roman takeover of Egypt in 30 BC. In about 300 BC the Egyptian priest Manetho wrote the first history of Egypt, dividing the list of kings into 30 **dynasties**, lasting from about 3100 BC to 332 BC.

The Old Kingdom (3rd – 6th Dynasty)

People in the Old Kingdom believed that only the king could survive death, since he was thought to be a god. During the 4th Dynasty, almost everyone in Egypt worked on the great smooth-sided stone **pyramids** and temples at Giza. The Old Kingdom ended in chaos after a series of **famines**.

The Middle Kingdom (11th – 12th Dynasty)

In the 11th Dynasty King Mentuhotep reunited the country. Trade was strengthened with Crete and Sinai, and the borders of Egypt were pushed south into Nubia. At the end of the 12th Dynasty the central administration broke down. Foreign rulers, called the Hyksos, took over Lower Egypt, bringing with them horse-drawn chariots, new weapons and musical instruments like the lute.

The New Kingdom (18th – 20th Dynasty)

During the New Kingdom there were two very unusual rulers. Akhenaten tried to change everything, creating a new religion and a new capital city at el-Amarna. The other was a woman called Queen Hatshepsut – unusual because the idea of a female ruler was unheard of. She ruled Egypt with great success, certainly as well as any of her male **predecessors**.

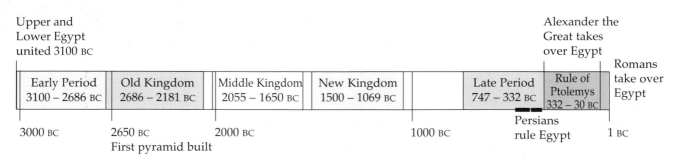

	Upper and Lower Egypt united 3100 BC						Alexander the Great takes over Egypt	
	Early Period 3100 – 2686 BC	Old Kingdom 2686 – 2181 BC	Middle Kingdom 2055 – 1650 BC	New Kingdom 1500 – 1069 BC		Late Period 747 – 332 BC	Rule of Ptolemys 332 – 30 BC	Romans take over Egypt
	3000 BC	2650 BC First pyramid built	2000 BC		1000 BC	Persians rule Egypt		1 BC

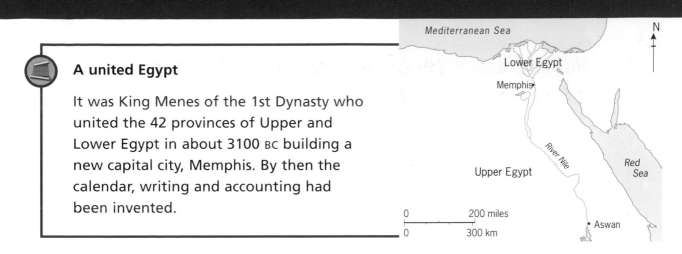

A united Egypt

It was King Menes of the 1st Dynasty who united the 42 provinces of Upper and Lower Egypt in about 3100 BC building a new capital city, Memphis. By then the calendar, writing and accounting had been invented.

The New Kingdom came to an end just before 1000 BC. Following this, in the Late Dynastic period (sometimes called the Late Kingdom), Nubians conquered Egypt but were driven out by the Assyrians a few years later, who were followed by the Persians, the Greeks and finally the Romans.

How do we know?

Most people know about ancient Egypt from looking at things that have survived from that time such as the treasures of the **pharaoh** Tutankhamun or ancient Egyptian **mummies**. We can also learn from the Egyptian writing, some of which survives in **tombs** and on the walls of buildings.

Tombs

Pharaohs were buried in rock-cut tombs here in the Valley of the Kings during the New Kingdom.

Exploring further

The Heinemann Explore CD-ROM will give you information about ancient Egypt. From the Contents screen you can click on the blue words to find out what we know about the ancient Egyptians.

What can we learn about ancient Egypt from one object?

Different objects tell us different things about ancient Egypt. It is important to look at as many **artefacts**, buildings and other remains from the time as possible. Each time you look at a photo of an Egyptian object, you should think about the things that the object tells us about the ancient Egyptians. Here are some questions to ask yourself about whatever you are looking at:

Who made it?

Was it made by a person with special skills, or could anyone have made it? Was it made by more than one person (like the **pyramids**) and if so would it have needed many different sorts of skills?

What was it made from?

Was it made from a precious and expensive material, like gold, or from a cheap material like wood?

What was it for?

Was it made as a practical tool (like a brick mould, a wooden hoe, a basket)?
Was it made as an ornament (like a necklace or earrings)?
Was it made to last (like the pyramids)?
Was it made for religious reasons (like the models found in **tombs**)?

Sometimes objects are made for more than one purpose. For example a beautiful glass jar for makeup is a practical tool, but it is also an ornament.

Tutankhamun

The **pharaoh** Tutankhamun ruled from 1336–1327 BC. He was nine years old when he began to rule. The country was really run by his two advisers, Ay and Horemheb, because Tutankhamun was so young. Tutankhamun died suddenly in 1327 BC and his body was **mummified**. He seems to have died from a blow to the head. Some historians suspect that Ay had Tutankhamun killed.

Have a look at the death mask of the pharaoh Tutankhamun. The gold in it weighs 10.25 kilograms. From it, we can say that:

- The ancient Egyptians thought highly of their pharaohs.

- They may have buried them with a lot of treasure. (It is unlikely they would make just one lovely thing if they thought possessions were important to take with you.) You would need to check if there was any other treasure found.

- The ancient Egyptians thought it was important to bury people carefully. The ancient Egyptians probably thought death masks should look like the dead person. (They have made this mask look quite young and we know Tutankhamun was a young man when he died.) The ancient Egyptians either traded for gold and precious stones or they were found in Egypt itself.

- The ancient Egyptians had very skilled craftsmen.

Exploring further – Tutankhamun's tomb

The tomb of Tutankhamun was discovered in the 20th century. To learn more about the people who discovered it, and the treasure they found, follow this path on the CD-ROM:

Contents > Exploring > Carter, Carnarvon and Tutankhamun's treasure

Click on one of the pictures on the left of the screen to make it bigger. The pictures show what was found in the tomb.

What does the landscape tell us about life in ancient Egypt?

Most people's lives are affected by the landscape and climate of the place where they live. This was especially true of the ancient Egyptians. Egypt is hot and dry all year round with very little rainfall. Land with no water is known as desert. Much of Egypt is made up of desert. Although water is needed to grow crops for food, the desert was still useful because its rocks held gold and precious stones.

Natural defences

The ancient Egyptians were lucky because Egypt had natural borders that cut it off from the rest of the world. Desert sands separated it from Sinai to the east and Libya to the west. The Mediterranean Sea, and the tangle of rivers and marshes in the Delta, lay between Egypt and Europe to the north. A huge waterfall at Elephantine, now called Aswan, stopped boats sailing to and from Nubia in the south. These natural defences made Egypt hard to attack.

The flooding of the Nile allowed farmers to cultivate the surrounding land – shown by the green shaded area.

8

Water in the desert

The River Nile runs the whole length of Egypt. The ancient Egyptians lived along the banks of the river. People travelled and moved goods by river. The river also meant they could grow food. Once a year, in ancient times, the Nile flooded. This time was called the **inundation**. When the river went down it left a thick layer of mud. This layer of mud was very **fertile** and provided good soil for crops to grow in.

The ancient Egyptians usually grew or made all the things they needed. They did not need to trade with other countries unless the Nile did not flood enough and farmers could not grow enough food. Then, the Egyptians had to trade for food – or starve.

A dry land

Without the Nile Egypt would be almost barren.

Exploring further – Egypt's borders

Egypt had strong natural borders, but other people still sometimes attacked them. Follow this path on the CD-ROM to find out more about Egypt's wars:
Contents > Exploring > Egypt's borders
Click on Written Sources on the left of the screen to see some of the writings that have survived to tell us about Egypt's wars.

How much of the life of ancient Egypt depended on the Nile?

Ancient Egyptians lived in towns strung out along the banks of the River Nile – they could not move far inland because the land became desert very quickly. The flooding of the River Nile, called the **inundation**, each year gave them the **fertile** soil they needed for farming.

Written evidence

Part of a song to the River Nile, written in about 2020 BC, which shows how important the inundation was to ancient Egyptians.

Lord of the fish, he sends the birds flying south
  as he rises,
He is father to the barley and the wheat.
If he is slow to rise, people hold their breath,
They grow fierce as food runs short and many
  starve.
When the flooding is absent greed stalks the land,
Rich and poor alike wander the roads, homeless.
Yet when the river rises, sparkling, the land
  rejoices,
Every stomach will be filled.

This is from some letters sent home by Hekanakhte. He was a **scribe** and priest, who had been sent to the Delta on official business in about 2000 BC.

How are you, are you alive and healthy? Don't worry about me, I'm alive. Now, the inundation isn't very high, is it? So keep to the list of rations below! Look, I've managed to keep you all alive up until now, so don't be angry about this. Being hungry is better than being dead altogether. You don't know real hunger – they are eating people up here.

The flooding also meant they had to build their settlements on higher ground, so that the fields were flooded but the towns were not. This meant that everyone who farmed lived in towns, rather than in the fields. The flooding also meant that the fields were underwater for several months. So farmers had other jobs too and most people helped with farming tasks like clearing the **irrigation** ditches and harvesting crops.

Measuring the river

How did the ancient Egyptians measure the inundation? They set up Nilometers along the River Nile. These were stone steps with stone walls down to the river at its lowest point. They cut marks into the stone sides. Scribes recorded the level of the water against these marks each year to see if the river was rising more slowly than usual. some Nilometers are still there.

Exploring further – The River Nile

To find more information about how the river affected life in ancient Egypt, click on Search on the top panel of the Contents page. Pick River Nile from the keywords on the next page and click on Enter. The screen will now show a list of pages on the CD-ROM that mention the River Nile. Click on the names of the pages to find out what they show.

What objects survive from the time of the ancient Egyptians?

The objects that have survived from ancient Egyptian times are mostly **tombs** and items put in burials with dead people. The ancient Egyptians believed in an **afterlife** that was just like everyday life, only perfect. This means that wall paintings in tombs that show farming scenes, for example, show proper tools and farming methods. However, they also show rich people farming in their best clothes and crops growing very well – to make things perfect.

Tomb models

This model of a typical Egyptian boat was found when a tomb was **excavated**. We can tell the size of the boat from the model people.

People were buried with many of their possessions (or models of those possessions that were too large to fit into the tomb). So we have good examples of everything people would have used in everyday life – from jewellery to farming tools to food and drink. This means that, even though we are looking at ancient Egypt from just one angle, we can get a good idea of what Egyptian farms, tools and possessions were like.

A few towns have survived too, allowing us to get an idea about ordinary homes and everyday life. However, when a town is found, it is only the stone bases of the houses that remain. The mud bricks the houses were built from have long since crumbled away.

Hekanakhte

Hekanakhte was a **scribe** and priest, who lived and worked in Thebes in about 2000 BC. He was not an important official and normally we would not know anything about him. Luckily, a set of his letters home, written when he was sent to the Delta on official business, has survived.

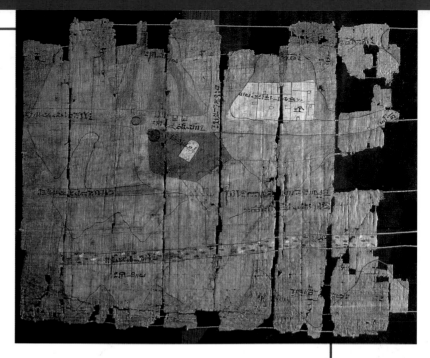

These give us a very rare look at an ordinary ancient Egyptian family. Hekanakhte's family and household consisted of:

- Hekanakhte
- Iutenheb – his second wife
- Five sons by his first wife - Merisu (the oldest, adult, in charge while Hekanakhte was away), Sahathor (next oldest, adult, with his father and carrying letters back and forth), Sanebniut, Inpu and finally Snefru (the youngest, spoiled by everyone)
- Ipi – Hekanakhte's mother
- At least two daughters – Hotepet and Nefret
- Senen – a maid
- Various other servants

From the letters, it is clear that the children of Hekanakhte's first wife do not like his new wife. Hekanakhte tells them that they should treat her better. Most of his letters are about how his land should be farmed. Because he is writing at a time when food was short, he also sends lists of the rations his family should eat.

Exploring further – a range of objects

The CD-ROM includes pictures of many of the objects that have survived from ancient Egypt. Follow this path: Contents > Pictures
Click on a picture to make it bigger and to read a caption telling you what it shows.

What do objects that have survived tell us about farming in ancient Egypt?

Paintings of farming scenes have been discovered on the walls of Egyptian **tombs** and some examples of crops have survived, dried in the desert sand. Today we can see them in modern museums.

The farming year

There were three stages to the ancient Egyptian farmer's year. The first stage was the **inundation**, when the River Nile flooded. This was from July to October. During the inundation, the land was underwater, so farmers mended tools and looked after their animals. Also, they had to work for the **pharaoh** for some days each year. This work was done during the inundation and was often building work.

The second stage was planting time from November to April. The mud was still soft and easy to plough. One farmer ploughed the soil. A second farmer followed him and sowed the grain. A third drove sheep or goats over the seeds to tread them into the soil. Once the grain was planted, the farmers **irrigated** it until harvest time in March. There was just time to grow a second crop of beans in the same fields.

The third stage took place in May and June after the second crop was harvested. Now it was time to clear the ditches and ponds around the fields. The ancient Egyptians tried to save as much water as possible from the inundation. They trapped the water in big ponds. They dug ditches all round the fields, with **sluice boards** to stop the water being wasted.

Other work

A tomb model of a weaving workshop shows us some of the other activities of the ancient Egyptians when they were not farming.

What did the ancient Egyptians farm?

As well as growing crops, farmers kept animals, mostly for food. Cows, sheep and goats were kept for meat and milk. The skins were used too. Ducks and geese were kept for eggs and meat. The Egyptians also caught fish and wild animals to eat. Bees were kept for honey, which was used to sweeten food and drink.

Pictures of farming scenes on tomb walls often include **hieroglyphs** of farmers talking with each other. Here is an example translated into English:

'A fine, cool day! The oxen are pulling the plough. The weather is good, let us work for the master.'
'Go on, guide it! Hurry, hurry you in front! Drive the oxen! Mind your feet. Watch out, the master's here and he's watching us!'

What do objects that have survived tell us about food in ancient Egypt?

Bread and beer were the most important foods in ancient Egypt. Both were made from grain. When the grain was ground up fine, it made bread flour. Beer was made from bread mashed up with water. It was left to settle, then strained into jars. It was very thick and quite weak – even children drank it.

Tomb models show beer-making. **Archaeologists** have found beer jars with remains in the bottom. Archaeologists who found the strainer were not sure what it was for. They worked it out when they found a tomb painting of a man drinking beer through a strainer.

The ancient Egyptians ate a lot of vegetables. They ate beans, onions, leeks, garlic, cucumbers and lettuce. The fruits they grew most were grapes, pomegranates, figs and dates. Meat was only for special occasions, unless you were rich. Rich people ate all kinds of animals, both wild and farmed.

Food and drink

It was assumed that people would need food to eat in the **afterlife**, so pictures or models of food were buried in the tomb. From this we can tell what the ancient Egyptian diet was like.

Houses

This clay model shows a typical flat-roofed Egyptian house.

Cooking food

People did not cook inside their homes. Large houses had a kitchen built away from the house. Ordinary people had ovens in their yards. Most other foods were cooked on open fires in yards or on the flat roofs of houses. Ordinary people often gathered and ate on the roof too. They shaded themselves from the sun by a linen sheet on poles.

From 'The Tale of Sinuhe', an ancient Egyptian story written in about 2000 BC. This passage tells us what ancient Egyptians thought of as luxury.

I was sent to rule the people in that beautiful place. Each day they brought me food; I drank wine every day – cooked meat, or roast duck or dishes of wild desert animals. They hunted for me and they fished for me, adding to the animals that my own greyhounds caught. They filled me with numberless sweet things, milk and many baked things

Exploring further – Food

Follow this path to discover more about food on the CD-ROM:
Contents > Exploring > Everyday Life > Food and drink
Click on the pictures on the left of the screen to find out what they show.
You could also use the Exploring further link on page 15 to find more information about food.

What do buildings that have survived tell us about ancient Egypt?

Towns

Archaeologists have found some ancient Egyptian towns. The mud bricks have crumbled away, but the stone bases for the houses are still there. Paintings and **tomb** models from the time also show houses.

Homes

Ancient Egyptians, and that includes the **pharaohs**, lived in houses made from mud bricks. Homes had thick walls and small, high windows, to keep out the heat. Light came in through air vents in the flat roof. People worked, cooked and ate on the roof. Even well-off people had very little furniture. Ordinary people sat on mats and slept on mud-brick sleeping shelves, raised off the ground.

Temples

Temples were built from stone. So many of them have survived. Temples were whitewashed, then painted with pictures and **hieroglyphs**. Much of the colour has worn off the walls and pillars, but some still remains and this gives us an idea of how brightly coloured they were.

Temples were made up of covered courtyards and rooms. All the priests could go into the main courtyard. But as they went from one courtyard to another, fewer and fewer priests could go on. Only the High Priest could go right into the god's central shrine.

Pyramids

The enormous **pyramids** at Giza were built as tombs for Egyptian pharaohs. Only the first pyramids were made of stone. Later ones were made from mud bricks. The biggest is the Great Pyramid, which was built for the pharaoh Khufu (also known as Cheops) in about 2500 BC. People still wonder how such enormous buildings could be made without modern technology. All the ancient Egyptians had were rollers, ropes, levers and many pairs of hands and feet.

Tombs

At the time of the New Kingdom period all pharaohs were buried in the Valley of the Kings, near Thebes. They were buried in tombs cut deep into the rock. Pharaohs' tombs had lots of tunnels, and these led to many rooms. The coffin of the dead pharaoh was in one room. His treasure and his dead relatives were in others. Once the tunnels were cut, the walls, floor and roof were decorated with paintings and carvings.

Painters drew a grid on the walls and made a rough drawing of everything. When this was right they painted the colours over the design. At least one drawing board has survived to show how painters worked. On it we can see the grid and drawings. Also, several tombs were not finished by the time the body was ready for burial. So the person was buried anyway. This means that the early, unfinished stages are still there for us to see.

Exploring further – Deir el-Medina

The picture on page 18 shows the town of Deir el-Medina. To find out more about this town, follow this path on the CD-ROM:
Contents > Digging Deeper > Builders and Craftsmen > Deir el-Medina

What does writing and art that has survived tell us about ancient Egypt?

The ancient Egyptians developed writing by about 3100 BC. Their first writing was picture writing, where people drew a picture of what they wanted to say. So a picture of a mat meant 'a mat'. In the new **hieroglyphic** writing, pictures showed sounds, as well as a thing. So a picture of a mat could still mean 'a mat'. But it could also mean a sound that was part of another word. Only 27 sounds had their own **hieroglyph**.

Egyptian writing

Hieroglyphs (right) were a very slow way of writing, so two other kinds of writing grew up. Hieroglyphs like those in the top picture were used for important things like the decoration of **tombs** or religious writings. Priests used a less complicated type of writing for religious writings, called **hieratic**, and an even quicker, easier, writing called **demotic** (bottom picture), was used for ordinary letters, lists and accounts.

We know about ancient Egyptian writing because hieroglyphs cover the walls of the tombs, temples and **pyramids**. But only a few examples of hieratic or demotic writing have survived.

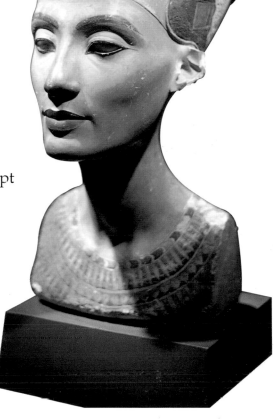

Egyptian queen

This statue is of the Egyptian queen Nefertiti from the 18th **Dynasty**.

Art and artists

Ancient Egyptian art has lots of detail and the colours are still bright after thousands of years. We can recognize it straight away. There are images of people, gods and goddesses, and pictures of everyday life. The models that were buried in the tomb with their owner bring everyday life in ancient Egypt to life for us now. They show people making bread and beer. They show them farming, sailing boats and counting animals.

The names of the artists whose works filled the tombs, temples and palaces of ancient Egypt are almost all lost because they did not sign their names. We know one name by accident – in one tomb scene he painted himself decorating a statue. An admirer later copied the painting and added his name: Houy.

Ancient Egyptian art has been very well preserved by the desert sands. Ever since the tombs were uncovered **archaeologists** have been studying the paintings and carvings inside them. But we will not be able to study the tombs forever. As soon as tombs are **excavated** and people start to visit them, the tombs get spoilt by air **pollution**, sweat and trampling feet.

Exploring further – Scribes

Find out more about how important scribes were in ancient Egypt. Follow this path on the CD-ROM to explore further:
Contents > Exploring > Everyday Life > Writing
Click on Written Sources to discover how scribes were trained.

What does technology that has survived tell us about ancient Egypt?

Irrigation

The River Nile was the only source of water in ancient Egypt. The ancient Egyptians invented ways of getting water from the Nile on to their fields. This is called **irrigation**. They dug lots of connected ponds and ditches, to trap the water. There were wooden **sluice boards** all along the ditches. When the boards were shut, the water was held back. When the boards were lifted, the water could move into the next ditch. The water was moved to exactly where it was needed and was not wasted. There are writings about the irrigation system that the ancient Egyptians used. It was important that they controlled the annual flood or their crops would fail.

The shaduf

During the New Kingdom, the ancient Egyptians began to use **shadufs** to lift water from the river. A shaduf is a long pole with a weight on one end and a bucket on the other. It is fixed to a frame on the river bank. A person pushes the pole so that it dips the bucket down into the water. The bucket fills with water. The person holding the pole then lets go and the weight on the end of the pole lifts the bucket up from the river. We know how shadufs work because they are still used in Egypt today.

Tomb walls

There are pictures of ancient Egyptian tools and technology on **tomb** walls. This carving shows one of the officials of King Zoser. He was chief of Dentists and Physicians and is pictured carrying the tools of a **scribe**.

Maps

As far as we know the earliest map was drawn in 1150 BC. It was of the gold mines at Wadi Hammamat. Before maps, people just asked the way. The ancient Egyptians also made maps of the sky. Priests needed sky maps to work out when to hold religious ceremonies. Some ancient Egyptian coffin lids had maps, but not maps of real places. The coffin maps show the dead person how to find their way safely into the **afterlife**.

Exploring further – Imhotep

Imhotep was a doctor, astronomer and architect. Read about the life of this remarkable man by following this path:

Contents > Biographies > Imhotep

What did the ancient Egyptians believe about life after death?

The ancient Egyptians believed in many different gods and goddesses. Paintings and statues of the gods often show them with human bodies and animal heads. The gods and goddesses controlled different parts of everyday life. The ancient Egyptians also had 'household gods' who they worshipped at small shrines in their home. **Pharaohs** were sometimes worshipped as gods.

The ancient Egyptians believed that people came back to life after they died on Earth and so needed their bodies and as many possessions as possible for the **afterlife**. Children had a duty to bury their parents properly so that they were comfortable in the afterlife. They prayed for their parents long after they had died and took food and drink to the chapels near their burial places. Couples that had no children often adopted some. A craftsman with no children would adopt one of his adult workers to take over his business.

The afterlife

The ancient Egyptians believed that the dead were judged by the gods and then lived in the 'Field of Reeds'. Here everything was like real life, only perfect. So, dead people needed their bodies to be preserved. The ancient Egyptians developed **embalming** as the best way of preserving a body.

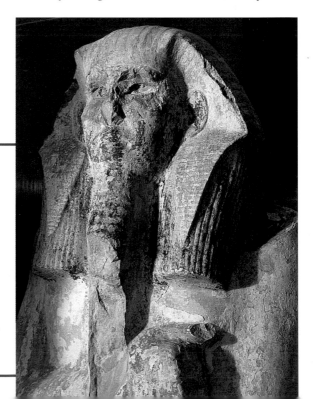

King Zoser

This statue of the 3rd **Dynasty** King Zoser was discovered at the burial complex at Saqqara. Zoser was buried in the first stone **pyramid** to be built. It is the oldest stone building still standing in Egypt.

Protection

Not only were people buried with all the possessions they might need in the afterlife, they were also sometimes protected by spells, like this one, painted onto their **tomb** walls.

People were buried with as many of their possessions as possible, like food, furniture, clothes and jewellery. Some things were too big to be buried with them, like houses, boats and grain stores, so models were made and buried with them. There were models of servants doing ordinary work. There were **shabtis** too. Shabtis were workers to do duty work, such as working on the pyramids for the pharaoh, for the dead person.

How do we know?

The paintings on tomb walls show life in the Field of Reeds and also burials. **Papyrus scrolls**, buried with the dead, show the owner of the tomb being judged by the gods. Tomb owners were always shown passing the judgement of the gods and being allowed into the afterlife!

Exploring further – Valley of the Kings

The CD-ROM contains lots of information about the Valley of the Kings, where the pharaohs of the New Kingdom were buried. Follow this path:
Contents > Digging Deeper > Valley of the Kings
Click on the words in blue to explore further.

Mummies

It was important to the ancient Egyptians that the body of a dead person was preserved in order for them to be able to take it with them into the **afterlife**. To do this they developed ways of **embalming** bodies.

First, the embalmers took out all the soft insides, the parts that would rot. Then they washed out the insides with a salty liquid. The body was then left soaking in natron, a kind of salt, for 70 days.

After 70 days, the embalmers washed and dried the body, then wrapped it in long strips of linen soaked in oil. It took about 350 square metres of cloth to wrap the average **mummy**. That's about 200 large bedsheets. Embalmers added small **amulets** to protect the dead person from evil spirits. Wrapped mummies were put in person-shaped coffins. Finally the coffins were given to the priests who led the burial ceremony in the nearby cemetery.

Tombs

The more important a person was, the more complicated his or her **tomb** was. A **pharaoh's** tomb had a series of tunnels that led to many rooms. Some of these connected up but others were dead ends. The tombs twisted and turned inside the hillside so as to confuse tomb robbers.

Cats

Cats were **sacred** in ancient Egypt. **Archaeologists** have discovered many embalmed cats like this mummy.

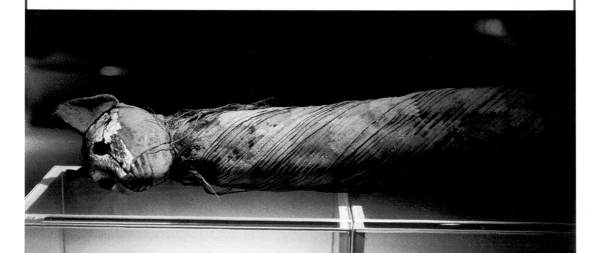

Often a person was ready for burial before the tomb was finished, so some tombs are unfinished. The pharaoh Tutankhamun died so unexpectedly that he had to be buried in a tomb intended for someone else.

How do we know?

These days scientists can use modern technology to examine mummies without unwrapping them. Using only a few strands of hair, or a few flakes of skin, they can find out the age and sex of the mummy and even what diseases they had!

Tomb treasures

From a tomb robber's confession made in about 1080 BC. Either the robbers never found the real treasure room or the tomb had been robbed before. Copper and coloured cloth do not sound like grand possessions for a pharaoh.

A villager showed us the tomb of Rameses VI, the Great God. The five of us spent five days breaking into the tomb. ... We found 60 chests and a basket on top of them full of things made from copper. We also found clothes, 25 garments of coloured cloth.

Exploring further – Mummies

Scientists can examine mummies to see what the ancient Egyptians used to preserve them for so long. Follow this path to discover what scientists have found:

Contents > Written Sources > Chemicals and colours

What can we learn about ancient Egypt from what has survived?

Studying the places and **artefacts** that have survived from ancient Egyptian times can tell us a lot about the ancient Egyptians and their beliefs. The dry desert sand has preserved bodies, **tombs**, even wooden farming tools that would have rotted away in most other climates.

Most of what we know about the ancient Egyptians comes from the findings of **archaeologists** who have dug up and explored **pyramids** and ancient Egyptian tombs, and studied the places and artefacts they have uncovered. This means that what we know has gaps in it – we can only study the things that have been found. Also, we have to interpret a lot of the evidence like **hieroglyphics** and writings before we can work out what it means.

Champollion

The Rosetta stone is a stone covered with Egyptian hieroglyphic and **demotic** writing, and some Greek writing. It was discovered near the town of Rosetta (Rashid), north-east of Alexandria in August 1799. Champollion, a French historian, worked out how to translate the hieroglyphics on the stone. Champollion's work has meant that we can now understand Egyptian writing, and so learn about life in ancient Egypt from writings like the Rosetta stone.

This tomb entrance in the Valley of the Kings is one of the many things preserved by the dry desert conditions of Egypt.

Even though many ancient artefacts can be studied, archaeologists agree over some ideas about ancient Egypt and disagree over others. For example, historians agree that the ancient Egyptians thought it was important to show their **pharaohs** as war leaders. They also agree that the ancient Egyptians fought wars, although they make the point that not all the battles that the pharaohs are shown fighting were likely to have happened. They also disagree over why these wars were fought. Some people think they fought simply to stop other countries invading Egypt – not to take over other lands. Other people think they fought to begin to build an empire.

Excavation diary

The archaeologist Howard Carter discovered Tutankhamun's tomb in 1922. He kept a daily record of the **excavation** of the tomb.

Nov. 1st: Removed the Royal Mummy. Placed it in the sun for a few hours. Heat of the sun had no effect on the tar-like substance that has stuck the mummy to the coffin.
Nov. 2nd: Found the heat of the sun was still no use in freeing the mummy from its coffin. So we will have to examine it here.

Exploring further – Lives of the Pharoahs

We know more about the pharaohs and important people of ancient Egypt than we do about ordinary people. In their tombs hieroglyphs tell us about them. The CD-ROM includes information about the lives of these people.
Follow this path: Contents > Biographies
Then click on the names of people to find out more.

Timeline

3100–2686 BC	Early Dynastic Period
c3000 BC	Upper and Lower Egypt united under one ruler, King Menes. New capital city Memphis built. Hieroglyphics developed as a written language.
2686–2181 BC	Old Kingdom Period
2500–2181 BC	Major Pyramid building period
2551–2528 BC	Khufu (also called Cheops) ruled
c2500 BC	Great Pyramid of pharaoh Khufu (Cheops) built at Giza
2181–2055 BC	First Intermediate Period – Egypt divided. Famine throughout Egypt. No pyramids built.
2055–1650 BC	Middle Kingdom Period. Mentuhotep (1986–1956 BC) reunites Egypt. Pyramid building began again, mostly mud brick, not stone – continued until about 1600 BC.
2000 BC	Hekanakhte living and writing. Full-time army set up. More and more people embalmed and buried in tombs.
1650–1550 BC	Second Intermediate Period – Egypt divided again. Hyksos seize power.
1550–1069 BC	New Kingdom Period. First evidence of the use of a shaduf to lift water. Pharaohs and royal family buried in rock-cut tombs in Valley of the Kings and Valley of the Queens, near Thebes – workmen's village, Deir el-Medina, built nearby.
1473–1458 BC	Hatshepsut, the female pharaoh, ruled
1352–1336 BC	Akhenaten ruled, built new capital at El-Armana
1336–1327 BC	Tutankhamun ruled
1327–1323 BC	Ay ruled
1323–1295 BC	Horemheb ruled
1184–1153 BC	Rameses III ruled
1150 BC	First known map drawn, of gold mines at Wadi Hammamat
1069–747 BC	Third Intermediate Period – Egypt divided again
747–332 BC	Late Dynastic Period – Egypt controlled by Libyans, then Nubians, Assyrians and Persians took over in turn
332–30 BC	Ptolemaic Period – Alexander the Great conquered Egypt and founded capital city Alexandria
c300 BC	Manetho writes the first History of Egypt
270 BC	Lighthouse built at Alexandria
51–30 BC	Cleopatra ruled
30 BC	The Romans take over Egypt and rule it with a Governor

Glossary

afterlife the ancient Egyptians believed that the dead came back to life in the afterlife – a place called the Field of Reeds, which was just like real life, but perfect

amulet a piece of jewellery that protects against evil or danger

archaeologist a person who looks for, digs up and studies things left from past times

artefact man-made items from the past

demotic shorthand version of hieroglyphic writing developed during the New Kingdom

dynasty a group of pharaohs. Manetho, a priest, divided the lists of kings into 30 dynasties.

embalming a way of stopping a body from rotting, usually by drying it out and wrapping it in strips of cloth

excavation the careful digging up of earth from an area by archaeologists, to find and study things from the past

famine a serious widespread shortage of food

fertile soil that is fertile is rich and good for growing crops

hieratic a simplified form of hieroglyphs used for everyday writing and record keeping

hieroglyphs the pictures and symbols (instead of letters) that represent sounds or whole words

hieroglyphics a form of picture writing – the word means 'sacred carving' in ancient Greek

inundation from July to October the River Nile floods and all the fields are under water

irrigation watering land by using man-made methods. In ancient Egypt, irrigation used a system of ponds, ditches and sluices.

mummies bodies of dead people that have been preserved, usually by embalming

papyrus a reed that grew in waterlogged land along the River Nile. The ancient Egyptians ate the young shoots, pulled up the fully-grown plants and used the stems to make boats, and used the inside pith to make paper.

pharaoh the king (or ruler) in ancient Egypt

pollution damage done to the environment by man-made waste

predecessor any person who has gone before, such as an ancestor

pyramid a building made from stone with triangular sides that rise up from a square base and meet together at one point. They were used as tombs.

sacred dedicated to a god or religious purpose

scribes the only people in ancient Egypt who could read and write – scribes ran the country for the pharaoh and also acted as priests

scroll a roll of papyrus used for writing on

shabti a little model of a worker put in the tomb of a dead person to do work in the afterlife

sluice board a board across a ditch that can be lifted to let water run out, or shut to keep it in

tomb a place where someone is buried

Index